HEAT

By Marcus Brotherton

MULTNOMAH PUBLISHERS® *SISTERS, OREGON*

FLIPSWITCH WARNING

FS — This book may contain thought-provoking content you probably didn't hear in Sunday school. It should be discussed and debated with family and friends. This book does not contain the answers to all your questions, but helps you ask the right questions. Some biblical material may be inappropriate and shocking for people who want to be comfortable.

YEAH

{03}

HEAT

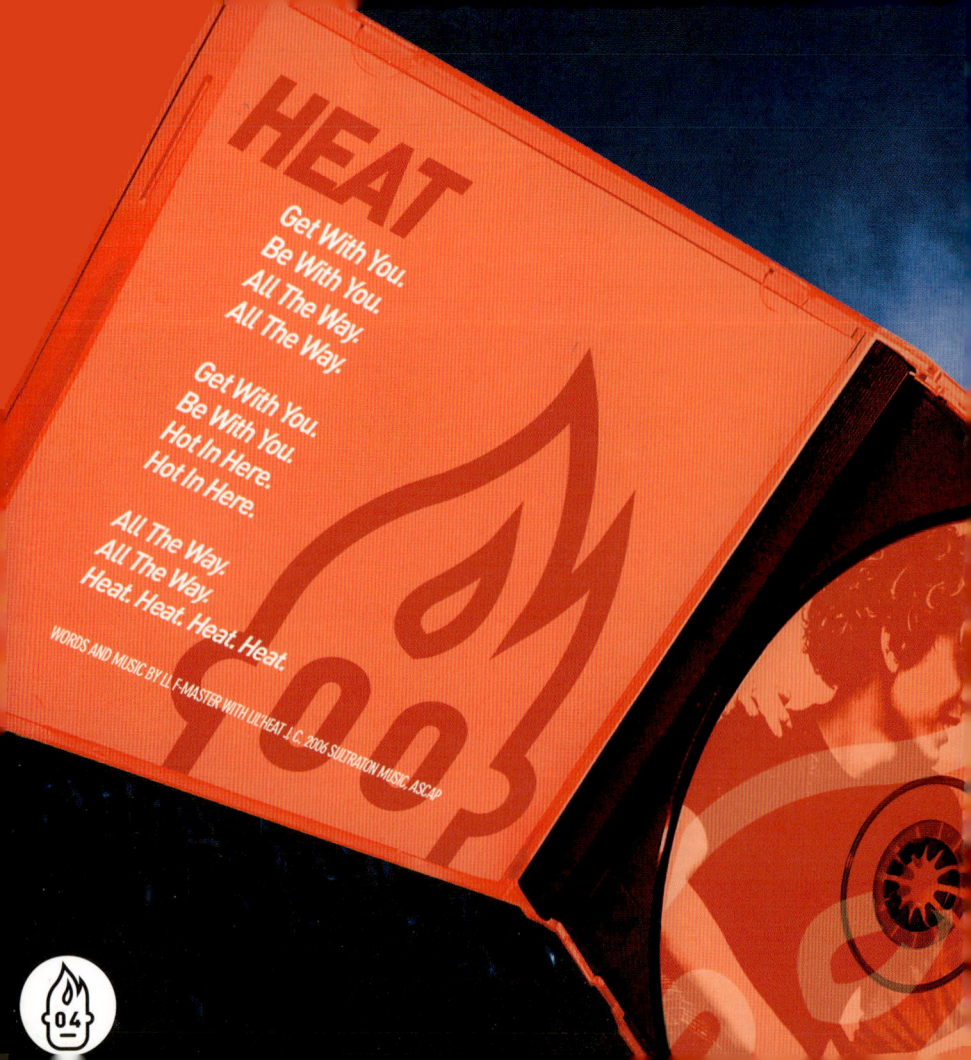

Get With You.
Be With You.
All The Way.
All The Way.

Get With You.
Be With You.
Hot In Here.
Hot In Here.

All The Way.
All The Way.
Heat. Heat. Heat. Heat.

WORDS AND MUSIC BY LL F-MASTER WITH LILHEAT J.C. 2006 SULTRATON MUSIC, ASCAP

04

Do you know me?
I know you.

I'm never far from you.
When you're waiting for the bus.
When you're walking down the hallway.
When you're sitting at your desk at school.

I both yell and whisper at you.
When you're lacing up your cleats on the soccer field.
When you're at the table before homework's done.
When you're under your covers at night.

You can't escape me.
I'm in a commercial on TV.
I'm in a song, downloaded off the Internet.
I'm in a sitcom, a movie, a magazine, a joke, a billboard.
I'm talked about on the phone.
I'm written about on notebooks.
I'm everywhere.
I'm everywhere.
I'm everywhere.

I'M HEAT.

05

MMM, I LOVE CHEESECAKE.

What if I was something completely random?

A bathtub maybe, or a big stinking cow? What if I was cheesecake? Can you imagine if everywhere you went, everything you saw, everything you heard, every message aimed your direction—said the same thing over and over again?

Mmm, I love cheesecake.

Try this: It's cheesecake.

There ain't nothin' better than cheesecake.

Have you heard the one about the cheesecake?

Eating cheesecake makes you cool.

Eating cheesecake makes you look sophisticated.

Eat your cheesecake today.

You aren't anything unless you're eating cheesecake.

Never tried cheesecake? Ha-ha-ha, I can't believe it. What a loser.

Cheesecake is sooooooo good.

I ate five cheesecakes last night.

She made him the best cheesecake over the summer.

The joy of cheesecake.

Cheesecakes gone wild.

Cheesecake, cheesecake, cheesecake.

IF YOU HAD NEVER TASTED CHEESECAKE BEFORE, and you were slammed with all this, would you not wonder, just a little, what all the fuss was about? And if cheesecake was something you knew about firsthand, and everywhere you looked was another message to eat cheesecake, wouldn't your appetite be whetted for even more?

That's the problem with HEAT these days. HEAT is everywhere. YOU CAN'T ESCAPE THINKING ABOUT HEAT, wondering about HEAT, and, for many of you, experimenting with HEAT.

fun with WISE HORSE and FACT-FRED carton head

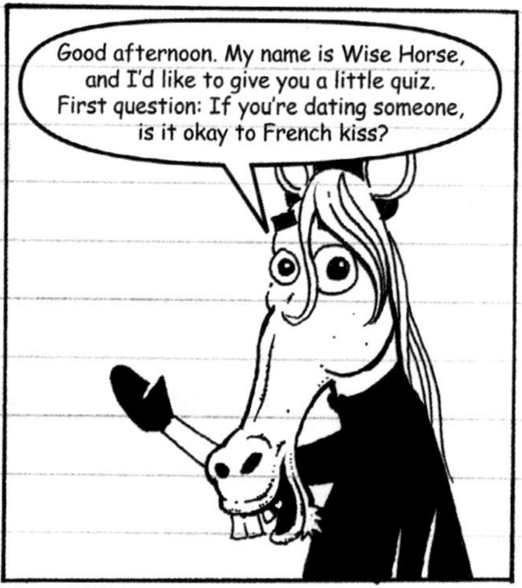

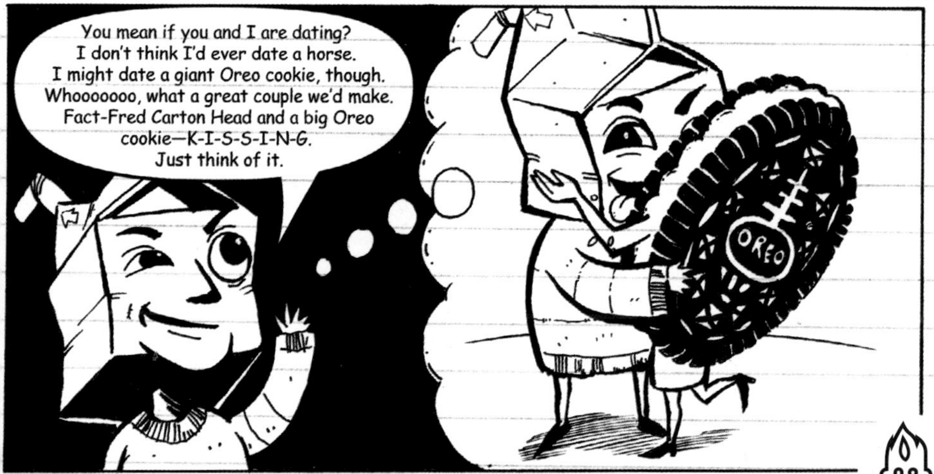

No. That's not what I had in mind. My intention with that question was to reveal some of the underlying conceptions you have about sexuality.
Hmmm. French kissing. Let me think. That hardly has anything to do with sexuality. Putting French kissing in the same category as sexuality is like putting your cousin in the lineup for potential prom dates.
This is a serious question. I want to know what you believe about the morality of (AHEM) open-mouth kissing. Is it right or wrong?
Well, Wise Horse, time for a fact or two.

The truth is, one hundred years ago we wouldn't have even been asking that question. It's not that people didn't French kiss back then; it's that teen sexuality really wasn't the issue it is today.
People are getting married later and later these days. The age that puberty begins has seriously declined over the years. Today we have girls getting their periods at nine or ten and boys able to do their part by age eleven or twelve.
Maybe it's all those hormones they put in hamburgers these days. Plumps up cows and then just zips you along too fast.
Another shot? Already? Yippee! I'm going to be sooooooo tasty when I'm grilled.
UBER HORMONE

Mayberry Cinema Productions, LLC

PRESENTS

What's Troubling Nancy and Harry?

AN EARL DANGLEMEYER FAMILY THEATRICAL EXPERIENCE
FOR YOUR VIEWING ENJOYMENT
C. 1957

*Popcorn, Sodas, and Other Fine Refreshments
Are Available in the Lobby.*

NANCY AND HARRY, *two fifteen-year-olds at West Valley High School, each had a problem. Nancy struggled with her grades in geometry, while Harry was cut from the basketball team.*

Gee whiz, Nancy, I'm so upset about not making the team. What would help me feel better is some illicit, premarital sexual intercourse.
What a keen idea, Harry! That will cheer me up about my geometry grade, too. Let's have relations tonight, right after the church social.

That's right, teenage friends. Nancy and Harry were both having sex for all the wrong reasons. And it can happen to you, too. If something goes wrong in your life, you may seek relief and pleasure as a means of feeling better. Wanting to feel better is not wrong. But the problem comes when you become sexually active as a means of masking some sort of pain in your life. Think about it for a moment. Has something like this ever happened to you?

Think a condom is the answer? One in Three will fail.

A report on condom effectiveness found that condoms have a 31 percent failure rate in preventing AIDS transmission. Condoms work slightly better in preventing pregnancy, but with stats like those, who wants to take a chance? Maybe condoms offer "safer sex," but definitely not sex without risk.

COLD HARD FACTS

THESE ARE THE COLD, HARD FACTS:

By age seventeen, five out of ten of us will be doing it.

5

17

AIDS/HIV
HEPATITIS A
HERPES
HEPATITIS B
GONORREHEA
PID
HPV
CERVICAL CANCER
SYPHILIS
MOLLUSCUM
CONTAGIOSUM
CHLAMYDIA
CRABS
SCABIES
NGU
CHANCROID
VAGINITUS/TRICHOMONIASIS

STD'S

Out of four, one of us will contract an STD this year.

19

Out of ten, two of us will get pregnant this year. One baby will be born. The other baby will be miscarried or aborted.

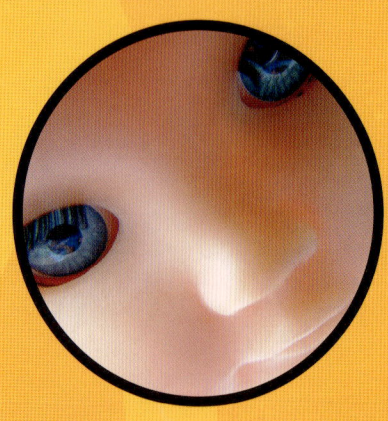

Each year almost one million teenage women—19 percent of those who have had sexual intercourse—become pregnant. That means about 2,800 teens get pregnant each day in the U.S. Out of all teen pregnancies, 56 percent give birth, 30 percent have an abortion, and 14 percent miscarry.

TWO OF US WILL GET PREGNANT THIS YEAR.

Nine ABSOLUTE Lies:

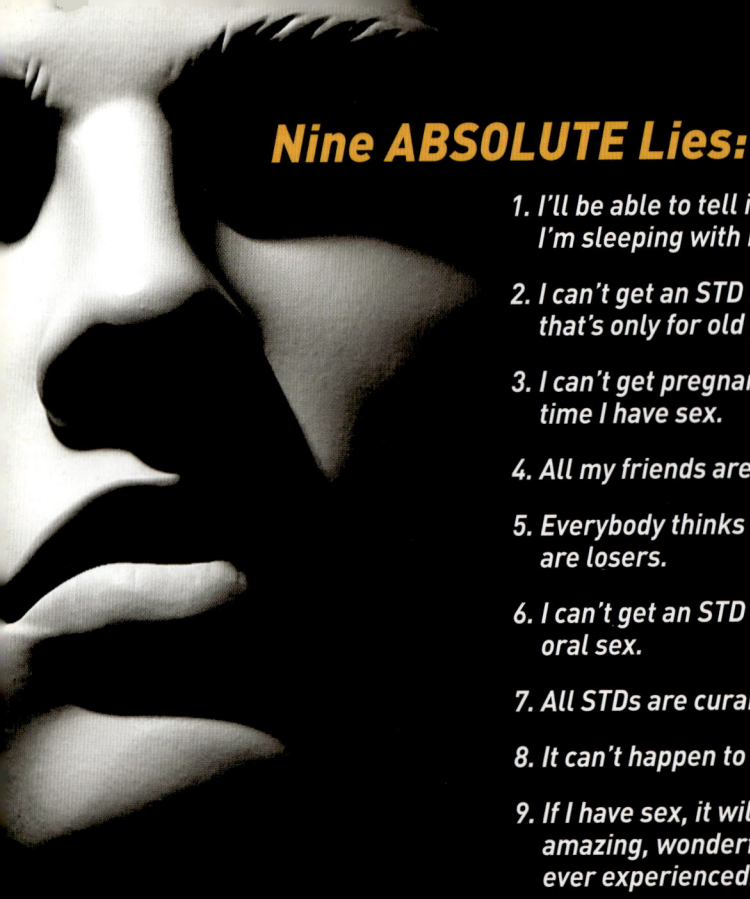

1. I'll be able to tell if the guy/girl I'm sleeping with has an STD.

2. I can't get an STD if I'm young—that's only for old people.

3. I can't get pregnant the first time I have sex.

4. All my friends are doing it.

5. Everybody thinks virgins are losers.

6. I can't get an STD from oral sex.

7. All STDs are curable.

8. It can't happen to me.

9. If I have sex, it will be the most amazing, wonderful thing I've ever experienced.

The Truth:

1. *Absolute lie. More than half of all people will have an STD at some point in their lifetime. Some STDs are "silent," causing no noticeable symptoms, and can be diagnosed only through testing.*

2. *STDs know no age limit. In the U.S. about one in four sexually active teens become infected with an STD every year.*

3. *First time. Second time. Fiftieth time. Doesn't matter. You can get pregnant every month regardless of whether it's your (or your partner's) first time to have sex or not.*

4. *Maybe, maybe not. At age fourteen, about one in ten teens has had sex. By the time you're fifteen, the numbers are still low—about three out of ten guys and two out of ten girls are having sex. By age seventeen, it's about half and half. Other stats show that it's actually becoming "cooler" to stay a virgin. More than half of all male high school students reported in 2001 that they were virgins, up from 29 percent in 1990.*

5. *Loser is as loser does. A study by* Seventeen *magazine and The Kaiser Family Foundation showed that the majority of you don't view virgins as losers. Of those surveyed, 92 percent said it's a good thing for a girl to be a virgin, and 81 percent said it's good for a guy to be a virgin.*

6. *Sorry, yes you can. Oral sex carries a significant risk for catching STDs, if either partner has one.*

7. No way. Some STDs can be cured through antibiotics. Some stay with you for your entire life. Some can weaken your immune system or cause other problems such as infertility in girls. Some can kill you.

"Should have waited."

8. Whatever.

9. Sex can be cool—that is no lie, but it's often not all it's hyped up to be. In one study of more than five hundred sexually active teens, more than half said they

REAL VOICES...

...of Hillary, age 15, in her diary (used by permission)

tonight, as i sat mesmerized by the mantel clock above my parents fireplace, ticking subconsciously in my brain, heard so many times by me its unheard now even, i began to wonder, this boy beside me, this boy holding my hand, this boy kissing my neck, this boy with his belt buckle so close to being undone, who he was, what he meant to me, what was all the confusion about, what did this decision in front of me mean in all naked, honest truth. i wish he would talk about these things more with me, i wish he would struggle in all passion and bewilderment like i do. this decision to do it or not. should i. should we. this decision is it. everything. it's what it's all about. how easy it would be right now... why hold on? my virginity is held by such a thin thread in this day and age. my mental virginity (if there is such a thing) is next to impossible—i think about it all the time. I know the bible says you cant have sex before marriage, but why cant you, if you're in love with the person? It doesn't feel wrong. but i really dont know if it feels right for me. sex seems so common. elaine and brittany and Kilee are so consumed by it anyway. the actual act almost borders on meaninglessness to me. he acts like he loves me but I wonder if sex is only a tonic for stress for him. or I'll put out so he wont leave me. whatever. sex is the common pastime. who wants to have a part in common? who wants to take part in what the rest of the world has already done? i dont know i just dont know

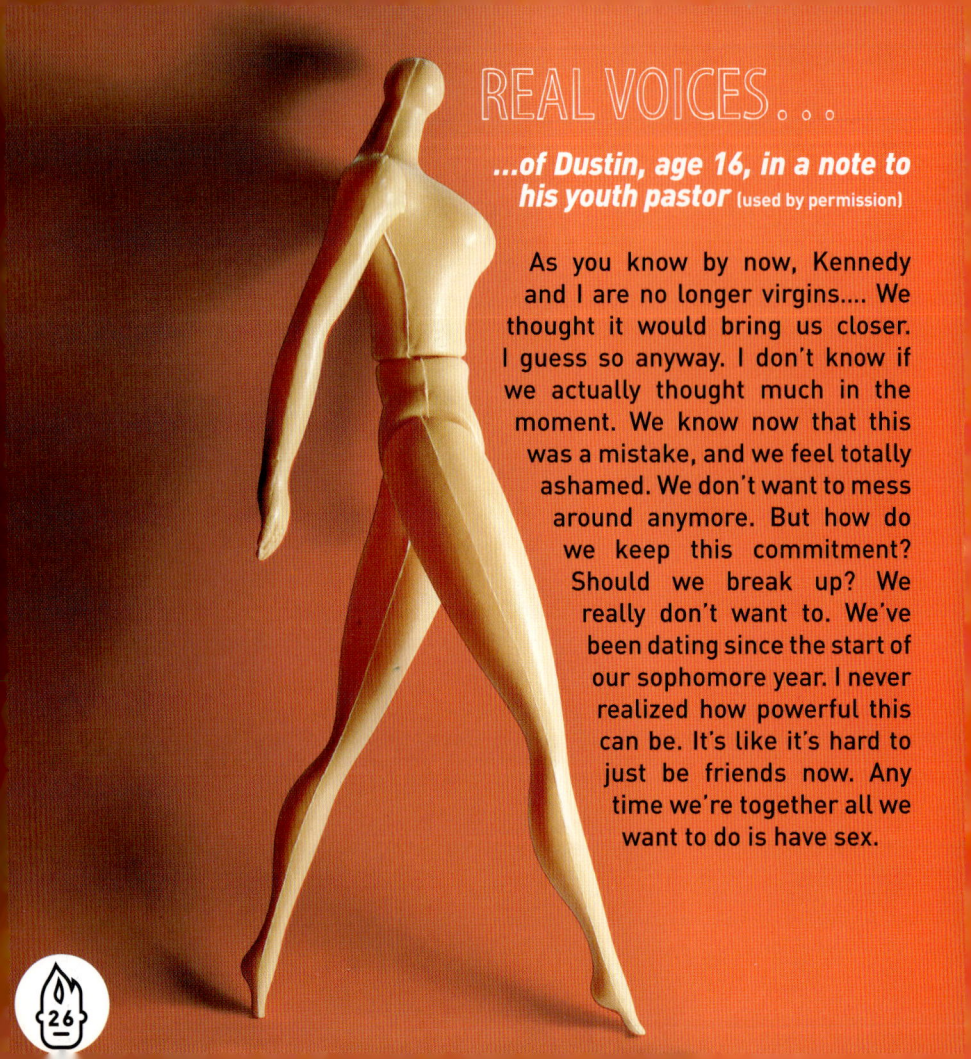

REAL VOICES...

...of Dustin, age 16, in a note to his youth pastor (used by permission)

As you know by now, Kennedy and I are no longer virgins.... We thought it would bring us closer. I guess so anyway. I don't know if we actually thought much in the moment. We know now that this was a mistake, and we feel totally ashamed. We don't want to mess around anymore. But how do we keep this commitment? Should we break up? We really don't want to. We've been dating since the start of our sophomore year. I never realized how powerful this can be. It's like it's hard to just be friends now. Any time we're together all we want to do is have sex.

REAL VOICES...

...of Nola, age 17 (public domain)

Blog 12/04

Emilio, bBAbe. You are so hot. Sometimes I can't believe we're together. I remember the first time I saw you when Natalie and me were down at gulianos pizza and you had just finished your shift...

Here is your poem I told you about yesterday. Can't say it to you yet anyway. please talk to me later. Text me. okay.

You are my sweetest laughter. You are my gentlest sleep. You are my turbulent RIVER. I love you so much. Why do I just want to sleep with you? My sex is Uncontrollable. I'm just Relentless. This White Water is large and unmapped, uncontrollable, Class 5 Rapids. I row my Kayak with eyes closed. What's it like?

Can't stop this. Can't turn this off. Can't just say wait. This relentless, pressing, running, demanding, kicking-up-a-storm child in the supermarket. RIVER. I'm kicking off my socks and shoes. Just want to wade into your RIVER.

Love,
Nola.

REAL VOICES...

...of Jeremy, age 18, in a letter to a friend (used by permission)

Elle wasn't a virgin when we started dating, but I was. She had decided in high school to have sex, just to try it. She had sex with four other guys before me. I've dated a couple of girls before, but they were virgins, too, and I just didn't feel as much pressure as I did with Elle. It was like she knew something I didn't. I used to wonder a lot what it was like. We fooled around bit by bit at first. We never planned to do stuff, but we found ourselves in places that just led to that. Like one time we were home alone and got to kissing on the couch. One thing led to another and then we found ourselves on my bed. Afterward I always vowed that we'd never do that again, but we always did. Sometimes I'd just think: We should just do it. Get it over with. Why not? So, eventually we did it. We only had actual intercourse two times. I felt angry with myself afterward. I've prayed, but I still don't feel forgiven.

FIND THE TRUTH

So do you have sex? Or don't you? If you don't have sex, how far can you go? Or if you've had sex, now what? How can you sift through all the questions and find answers? Find the truth?

The days of "the birds and bees"—where people just talked about sex in roundabout ways—are all over. We live in a real world that talks about, thinks about, and wonders about sex out loud. And we want real answers.

The Bible takes a strong position on sex. God's all for it. Does that sound strange to you? God is not against sex. Truth is He's the One who invented sex in the first place. God wants the best for you in all areas of your life—that includes your sexuality. But a lot of harm can come from sexual activity, too. And God doesn't want that for you.

Think of God's views on sex as an invitation to a party. But it's not just any old party. God says: Here's something that's incredibly pleasurable—I want you to enjoy it. But you need to show up to the right party at the right time at the right place. *How do you get to this party?*

FLIP HERE.

HEAT
BUZZ

www.flipswitch.com

flipswitch
flipswitch

BLUR
SPLIT

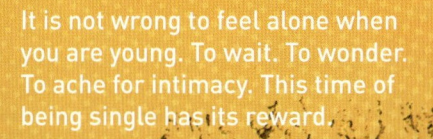

It is not wrong to feel alone when you are young. To wait. To wonder. To ache for intimacy. This time of being single has its reward.

When you find the one, after that season of not knowing, your love for that person will be all the more desirable, all the more precious, all the more appreciated, all the more wanted, all the more cherished, all the more held close.

LONG WAIT PART OF GIFT.

Within your reach...

A story is told of the son of missionaries who grew up in a small village in Tanzania. In the village was a well that bubbled up with the freshest, sweetest water for miles around. After the boy grew up, he often thought about that water and how good it tasted. Only one problem: He had become a missionary himself and now lived in Zambia, hundreds of miles away from his home village.

One of the young Zambians who worked with the missionary decided to do something about this. It was the missionary's birthday in a month, and the young Zambian began to dream up a way he could get his friend the perfect present.

On the morning of the missionary's birthday, he was greeted by a colorfully wrapped jar of well water. The missionary opened it and drank deeply. He could taste in an instant it was water from the village where he had grown up. Somehow, the young Zambian had come through.

"How did you ever get this water?" the missionary asked. "The price of train tickets is too steep."

"I walked," said the young Zambian.

"But the village is hundreds of miles away."

The young Zambian smiled.

"LONG WALK PART OF GIFT."

The good news is the struggle to live sexually pure is one you don't face alone.

Your sexual purity depends on two things:

1. The choices you make
2. The power of the Holy Spirit at work in your life

Living by the power of the Holy Spirit means you ask for God's help. You rely on Him to work in you. You don't ignore your responsibility, but you trust that He will help you live as you're meant to live. In freedom.

"So I say, live by the Spirit, and you will not gratify the desires of the sinful nature." **GALATIANS 5:16**

What does it mean to live by the Spirit?

It means that God is on our side. When we live in His house, we live in a house of love, not a house of fear. With the work Christ did for us on the cross, we are already completely pure in His sight. Jesus Christ is the One who makes us holy. It's by His power and grace that we live, not by a bunch of rules that we try to follow. Our invitation is to yield our lives to Him. How do we do that? It may start with the following prayer:

PRAYER:

God, I desire sexual purity in my life. I admit I cannot do this alone. Only by Your power do I have the ability to make the decisions I need to make. Help me in this area. Thank You that You make me pure. Thank You that I don't have to face this alone. I turn my sexuality over to You. Thank You for Your freedom. Amen.

Living sexually pure means that you are still a sexual person. But you choose to respect your code. Your code doesn't rob you of enjoyment. Actually your code gives you more freedom. By following what you ought to do, you can do what you truly want to do.

What do you want to do?

RUN. PLAY FOOTBALL. DANCE. SKATEBOARD. SNOW SKI. WINDSURF. HITCHHIKE **THROUGH NEPAL. JET SKI. WRITE. PLAY GUITAR. ROLLERBLADE. READ MAGAZINES.** PAINT. ACT. SING. PLAY BASEBALL. PLAY VOLLEYBALL. PLAY SOCCER. WATER-SKI. **ARCHERY. RIDE HORSES. JUMP IN A HOT TUB. READ BOOKS. SWIM. RIDE DIRT BIKES. PLAY HACKY SACK.** PLAY DRUMS. EAT LUNCH. EAT A SNACK. PLAY MONOPOLY. ACE YOUR SATS. COLLECT **BUGS. GO TO THE BEACH. CRANK UP YOUR STEREO REALLY LOUD. THROW DARTS. HANG** WITH BONO. TEXT MESSAGE A FRIEND. BAKE A CAKE.

And yeah.

HAVE SEX SOMEDAY WHEN YOU GET MARRIED.

As servants of God we commend ourselves in every way: in great endurance; in troubles, hardships and distresses; in beatings, imprisonments and riots; in hard work, sleepless nights and hunger, in *purity...*

WHOA. Did Paul just put *"purity"* in the same category as all those other hard things? Read that list again...

...in great endurance; in troubles, hardships and distresses; in beatings, imprisonments and riots; in hard work, sleepless nights and hunger, in *purity...*

YEP.
NOBODY SAID THIS WAS EASY.

59

Sometimes purity feels like...

EASIER-SAID-THAN-DONE THINGS IN LIFE:

1. Swimming the Pacific Ocean with handcuffs on
2. Climbing Mount Everest wearing only a T-shirt, shorts, and tennis shoes
3. Eating an entire whale for lunch. No mustard
4. Making a million dollars from a lemonade stand
5. Living a sexually pure life

Why can purity feel so difficult sometimes? It's not impossible when it comes to number five. But the apostle Paul certainly paints a tough picture of living sexually pure. Check out 2 **CORINTHIANS 6:4–6**

If you've blown it,

THERE IS NOWHERE TO GO BUT FORWARD...

Have mercy on me, O God, according to your unfailing love; according to your great compassion blot out my transgressions. Wash away all my iniquity and cleanse me from sin. **PSALM 51:1–2**

Come near to God and He will come near to you. Wash your hands, you sinners, and purify your hearts, you double-minded. Grieve, mourn and wail.... Humble yourself before the Lord, and He will lift you up. **JAMES 4:8–10**

If we confess our sins, he is faithful and just and will forgive us our sins and purify us from all unrighteousness. **1 JOHN 1:9**

"I will forgive their wickedness and will remember their sins no more." **JEREMIAH 31:34**

What happens in your soul...if you've blown it? Having sex is more than just physical. Sexual sins can hurt inside. And sometimes those feelings last.

Kelly, age 19
"After we had dated for a while, I sensed him starting to pull away from me. I didn't want him to break up with me, and I found myself doing things I never thought I would, just to keep him close."

Isaac, age 18
"I have this friend who would always say: 'Dude, it's not about losing your virginity. It's about gaining your sexuality.' But what a crock that was. I did feel like I lost something. And what I gained wasn't all I hoped it was."

Chris, age 19
"I was sexually abused when I was young, and so was my girlfriend, Alana. Having both been through that—it's like a bond. It can draw you so close to another person when you date. Having sex was like a decision we made—we were both going to have sex on our own terms this time. The trouble is, whatever pain you feel that night you still feel the next morning."

Mercedes, age 15
"Sometimes it feels like sexual sin is the unforgivable sin. It just never goes away. I think you've got to know the seriousness of sin, yes. But also, be gracious with yourself."

3. What places on a boy's/girl's body will I not touch before marriage?
The rule of thumb is as simple as this: What areas are covered by a bathing suit? That's probably a good sign they should be kept private until marriage.

4. Will I French kiss? Will I make out?
People used to think these were fairly innocent practices. But where do these behaviors get you besides horny and frustrated? Why not set some strong boundaries in this area?

5. Will I even date seriously?
Everybody dates—don't they? Well, no, not really. Lately, there's been a strong movement away from serious dating and all the trappings that go along with it. The movement leans toward friendship with the opposite sex until the age when you're ready to marry, and then courtship—or supervised interaction until the marriage date. When you think about it, dating can only go one of two ways: You either break up or you get married. So, particularly when you're in high school and marriage is years away, why date if you don't have to? For an in-depth look at this see Joshua Harris' book *I Kissed Dating Goodbye*.

THE POINT:
How stupid is it to wait until you're overwhelmed with temptation before you make decisions about your purity? Another piece of the code is safeguarding your life. Safeguarding takes courage. It also takes wisdom. Start by asking yourself honest questions and making solid decisions—right now. Choices like...

1. What personal qualities are absolutely necessary for the boy/girl I date?

If you're a Christian, the Bible is clear that you only marry another Christian (**2 CORINTHIANS 6:14**). That's actually for your benefit—you will want to share what's important to you with the one you love. So why become involved in a serious dating relationship with a non-Christian? Also, **GALATIANS 5:22-23** describes a person whose life is filled with the Holy Spirit. Does the person you're dating (or the person you want to date) have a life that's characterized by love, joy, peace, patience, kindness, goodness, faithfulness, gentleness, and self-control?

2. Where will I/won't I be alone with my boy/girlfriend?

It may be okay to be at school, at youth group, and at the mall together. But not in the backseat of his car, in your bedroom with the door shut, or in your favorite park behind a grove of trees. Why go there?

Obvious Question # 244:

When is the best time to decide how far is too far?

a. When you're making out on your boyfriend's bed when his parents aren't home.

b. WAY BEFORE IT EVER COMES TO THAT.

Think of filtering as an ounce of prevention. Too often the stuff we fill our minds with becomes the breeding ground for behavior later on that the Lord cannot bless. Out-of-control sexual activity can start with the TV shows we watch, the video games we play, the websites we visit, the magazines we read. It's not that all this stuff is the enemy—we don't have to avoid the world we live in—but if we let it stream into our lives unfiltered, it can fill our minds and hearts with garbage.

THINK ABOUT SUCH THINGS

Turn it off, throw it away, don't pick it up, don't have it in the house, put the locks on.

One important piece of the code that leads to freedom is filtering. Just like a filtered bottle of water tastes the best, filtering your surroundings helps lead to your freedom. When you filter you learn how to discern—you can tell the difference between good stuff and gunk, and you choose one over the other.

So, a little kid *(someone without discernment)* sees any old movie that looks cool and says:

I MUST WATCH IT NOW! NO MATTER WHAT IT SAYS! NO MATTER WHAT MESSAGE IS BEING PRESENTED! ALL THE OTHER LITTLE KIDS ARE WATCHING IT!

The Bible shows this piece of the code in **PHILIPPIANS 4:8**:

Finally...whatever is true , whatever is noble, whatever is right, whatever is pure, whatever is lovely, whatever is admirable—if anything is excellent or praiseworthy—think about such things.

51

Question:

Which bottle of water will go down more smoothly?

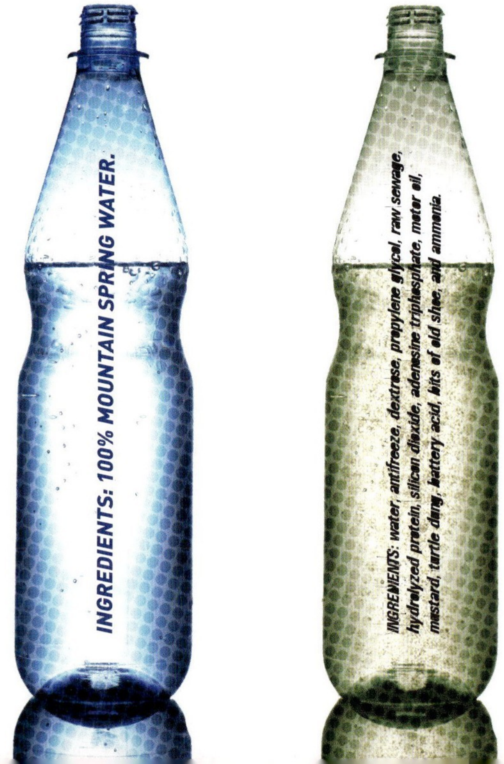

WELCOME TO Freedom
(Just Respect the Code)

True sexual freedom is when you have the maturity to accept limitations. You've developed a "code" to live by—a system of choices that allows your freedom. Your code has limitations built into it, but these limitations don't crush you. Your code doesn't limit your enjoyment. On the contrary, it actually gives you more. By following what you ought to do, you can do what you truly want to do. And that's what almost nobody tells you when it comes to living sexually pure...

RESPECTING THE CODE GIVES YOU FREEDOM.

Think of it this way...

Only when you respect the code for building a boat and learning to sail, can you stay afloat and whisk along the horizon, powered only by the wind.

Only when you respect the code for football—for learning how to throw a spiral and correctly block, tackle, and punt—can you truly play the game.

Only when you respect the code for driving—for staying on one side of the road, for stopping when a light is red and starting when a light is green—can you get where you need to go.

Only when you respect the code for chastity and morality can you live in true sexual freedom.

True freedom begins with paradox.

True freedom does not mean doing all you want. Only little kids do that. They get mad, so they yell and scream. They get tired, so they flop down on the ground. They want a toy, so they push and grab to get what they want. Children have not yet developed the maturity to accept limitations. They only live to satisfy their desires. Little kids are not truly free. They can't live how they truly want.

True freedom means doing what you ought. True freedom is maturity. Only by doing what you ought to do can you do what you really want to do. That's the paradox. To do what you ought means you need to make choices to bring that about, and accept the limitations those choices bring.

To choose one thing means you do not choose another. You can choose to play basketball, be in band, and work at a burger joint after school, or you can choose to play volleyball, run track, and be on the debate team—you won't have time for all these things. You can wear jeans to school, or you can wear a dress—one or the other. *You can drive a Ford or a Chevy—the choice is yours.* To say yes to one is to say no to another.

> "Freedom begins...not with doing what you want, but with doing what you ought."
>
> —ELISABETH ELLIOT, Author and speaker

FREEDOM

Mostly, the Bible describes purity as the knowledge that God created you for intimacy—fully knowing, fully known—with one other person for the rest of your life. When we're pure, we're at the party. When we're pure, we're free.

2 TIMOTHY 2:20–22 says: *In a large house there are articles not only of gold and silver, but also of wood and clay; some are for noble purpose and some for ignoble. If a man cleanses himself from the latter, he will be an instrument for noble purposes, made holy, useful to the Master and prepared to do any good work. Flee the evil desires of youth, and pursue righteousness, faith, love and peace, along with those who call on the Lord out of a pure heart.*

God is saying we're meant to live a life of noble purpose. The key for usefulness is being clean, not getting bogged down with "the evil desires of youth."

The Bible takes a very strong stance on sexual immorality.

1 THESSALONIANS 4:3–5: *"It is God's will...that you should avoid sexual immorality; that each of you should learn to control his own body in a way that is holy and honorable, not in passionate lust...."*

How do we live pure lives?

How do we learn to live a life with a noble purpose?

How can we live as sexually pure people?

KEEP READING...

When we're pure, we're free.

say about ? sexuality

The Bible talks about Joseph, a young man of 17. He's handsome and well-built, and while working as a slave in the palace of Potiphar, Joseph is propositioned by Potiphar's wife. "Come to bed with me," she says. But Joseph refuses. "How could I do such a wicked thing and sin against God?" Joseph asks. Life gets harder for Joseph because he takes a stand for purity. But in the end, it's one of the best decisions he ever makes (see **GENESIS 39**). The Bible talks about Solomon, the wealthiest and securest king Israel has ever seen. Solomon does great things with his life, but his addiction to sex is one of the things that eventually leads to his downfall and does him in (see **1 KINGS 11**).

What does the Bible

What else does the Bible teach about sexuality? The Bible is too much of a real book to just focus on simple slogans. In Scripture, instead of just giving us list after list of things we should or shouldn't do, God often talks to us through stories and examples of authentic people. These stories show us the choices that lead to harm, as well as the choices that lead to good.

I praise you because I am fearfully and wonderfully made; Your works are wonderful, I know that full well. My frame was not hidden from you when I was made in the secret place. When I was woven together in the depths of the earth, your eyes saw my unformed body.... Search me, O God, and know my heart; Test me and know my anxious thoughts. See if there is any offensive way in me, and lead me in the way everlasting.

The next time you shampoo up, take that piece of paper into the shower with you. Read that portion of Scripture out loud in the shower as you stand, naked. *(Bet you haven't done that before.)* The emphasis is not so much that you have no clothes on; it's that God completely knows everything about you. Everything. You are unclothed, uncovered, unprotected, unguarded before the Lord.

And you have nothing to worry about. GOD LOVES YOU SO MUCH. There are no barriers between you and God. God is your creator. He designed you.

HE THINKS THE WORLD OF YOU.

Let that thought push what you know about God over the edge.

Do you really believe that God created you as a sexual being, and that it's a good thing?

It's one thing to say that, and another to actually know it—to feel it in the depths of your soul where it really changes your life. The following may sound strange, but it's written with a purpose in mind. This may completely change what you think about God. Just give yourself to the moment and try it with an open mind...

Write out the words to PSALM 139: 1-4, 13-15, 23-24 on a piece of paper.

O Lord, you have searched me and you know me. You know when I sit and when I rise; you perceive my thoughts from afar. You discern my going out and my lying down; you are familiar with all my ways. Before a word is on my tongue you know it completely, O Lord.... For you created my inmost being; you knit me together in my mother's womb.

Quote that makes you go Hmmmmm...

"Sensuousness is no sin, but, on the contrary, an adornment to life—a gift of God, like the sweet winds of spring and summer. We should enjoy it with clear conscience and gladly, and should wish it to all healthy full-grown men and women who want it and need it."

—GUSTAV FRENSSEN, author

Question:

Is it okay to ever think about sex?

Answer:

GOD DOES.

Knowing this doesn't mean we can think about any sexual thing we want whenever we want. (Jesus says in Matthew 5:28 that if we even look at people lustfully, we've committed adultery in our hearts.) But the point here is that not all sexual thoughts we have are wrong. Actually, the opposite is true. We're sexual beings. We were created to have sex and enjoy sex. God invites us to think about sex—sex as it's presented within Scripture. Sex is good. But sex is powerful—so powerful it's got to be held within the bounds of one man, one woman, as long as they live. That's what God thinks about sex.

Do not arouse or awaken love until it so desires. **SONG OF SOLOMON 2:7**

God believes love cannot be forced. ***It must be patiently waited for.*** God also knows the power in sexuality. If sexuality isn't aroused in us, that's okay. Just leave it, God says.

I slept, but my heart was awake. Listen! My lover is knocking.... My lover thrust his hand through the latch-opening; my heart began to pound for him. **SONG OF SOLOMON 5:2, 4**

Sexuality involves intense emotions. God says it is not to be played around with. ***Sex is fun, but it's serious, too.*** Intense emotions need the boundaries of trust and safety that only marriage can offer.

We have a young sister, and her breasts are not yet grown. What shall we do for our sister for the day she is spoken for? If she is a wall, we will build towers of silver on her. If she is a door, we will enclose her with panels of cedar. **SONG OF SOLOMON 8:8–9**

Here, some older brothers are looking out for their younger sister's sexuality, as was often the case in Eastern families that had lots of kids. The brothers are asking, "What will happen when someone wants to marry our sister?" Their answer goes two ways. If she is like a wall, straight up and down, with steadfast and firm character, they'll reward her with honor and bless her marriage. If she's like a door, moveable and open to advances, they'll curb her behavior. God is saying that sexuality is a responsibility. ***It's a gift, but it's got to be used in the right ways.***

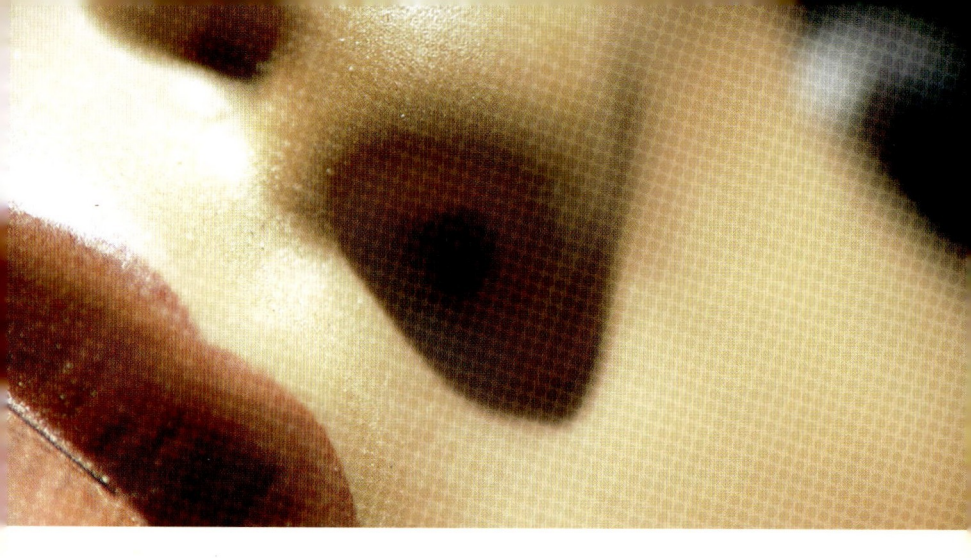

A BEAUTY ONLY GOD COULD DREAM UP

What does God think about sex? Just read the following passages taken from Song of Solomon...

We rejoice and delight in you; we will praise your love more than wine.
SONG OF SOLOMON 1:4

God is saying here that sex is something to rejoice in. It's a good thing—better than a strong, refreshing, intoxicating drink. Sex is powerful and exciting.

"Your breasts are like clusters of fruit," what it really means is that the Church is like a big baby and it needs a mother's milk to nourish it. Um... okay... Song of Solomon does give us a picture of true love, and Christ does love the Church. But the book is about much more than that. ***It's about sex.*** There is no other way to say it. God devotes an entire book in the Bible to this topic. ***Sex. Sex. Sex.*** Still, it's not the easiest book to read. It's tough to follow the plot or to know who's talking to whom. It can seem out of order. Really, Song of Solomon is like one long ancient poem—sort of like the Odyssey or the Iliad. But don't let that scare you off. It's kind of like a movie played out in different acts or scenes. Song of Solomon is the type of true, steamy drama we seldom get in today's movies. It's different because it's pure. It's not here to sell us stuff or ramp us up. ***It's here to show a type of beauty only God could dream up.***

Song of Solomon is one crazy book. It's an entire portion of Scripture dedicated to sex. In the Bible! In ancient Hebrew culture, you weren't even allowed to read Song of Solomon until you were thirty years old.

Today, you can read it at any age, but even so, how often do we flip through Song of Solomon on our own? Or when was the last time you heard a sermon in church from this book? Or memorized verses from Song of Solomon? Have you ever done your devotions out of Song of Solomon?

But why not? There's an amazing verse in the Bible that puts crazy portions of Scripture into a new light for us—**2 TIMOTHY 3:16** says all Scripture is useful. How much of Scripture is useful? All. That means Song of Solomon is here for a reason. God wants us to read it. To study it. To hear talks in youth group about it. To do our devotions from it. This is God's word on the subject of sex.

ALL SCRIPTURE IS USEFUL

Fifty years ago, when Christian scholars taught from this book, they tended to turn it into one big figure of speech—like, it wasn't really sex between a man and a woman that God was talking about—it must be just love. Yeah. That's it. Love—and Song of Solomon is actually only about the love between Christ and the Church. So when it says,

The Lord of all creation, in His perfect holiness, designed Adam and Eve as living, breathing, amazing sexual beings. God designed sex with absolutely pure motives—He wanted people to experience incredible beauty and joy. He wanted people to desire to have babies and take actions that would bring that about. He wanted people to be able to be intimately close to one another—so He designed body parts that fit together perfectly. God designed Eve with breasts, a vagina, and a clitoris. God designed Adam's penis to have an erection. Sometimes today we think about body parts as dirty or shameful, but God didn't design bodies that way. God designed naked bodies to be spectacular. ***For this reason a man will leave his father and mother and be united to his wife, and they will become one flesh.*** GENESIS 2:24

True sex is this: God designed one man and one woman to be naked and unashamed around each other—to delight in each other. God also designed one man and one woman to be with each other for their lifetimes—to leave their parents and stick to each other and become so close it's almost like they become one person. That's the "one flesh" bit. That's what sex started as:

ONE MAN. ONE WOMAN. UNITED AS ONE FLESH.

And God called His creation "good."

Part two of HEAT *begins here*

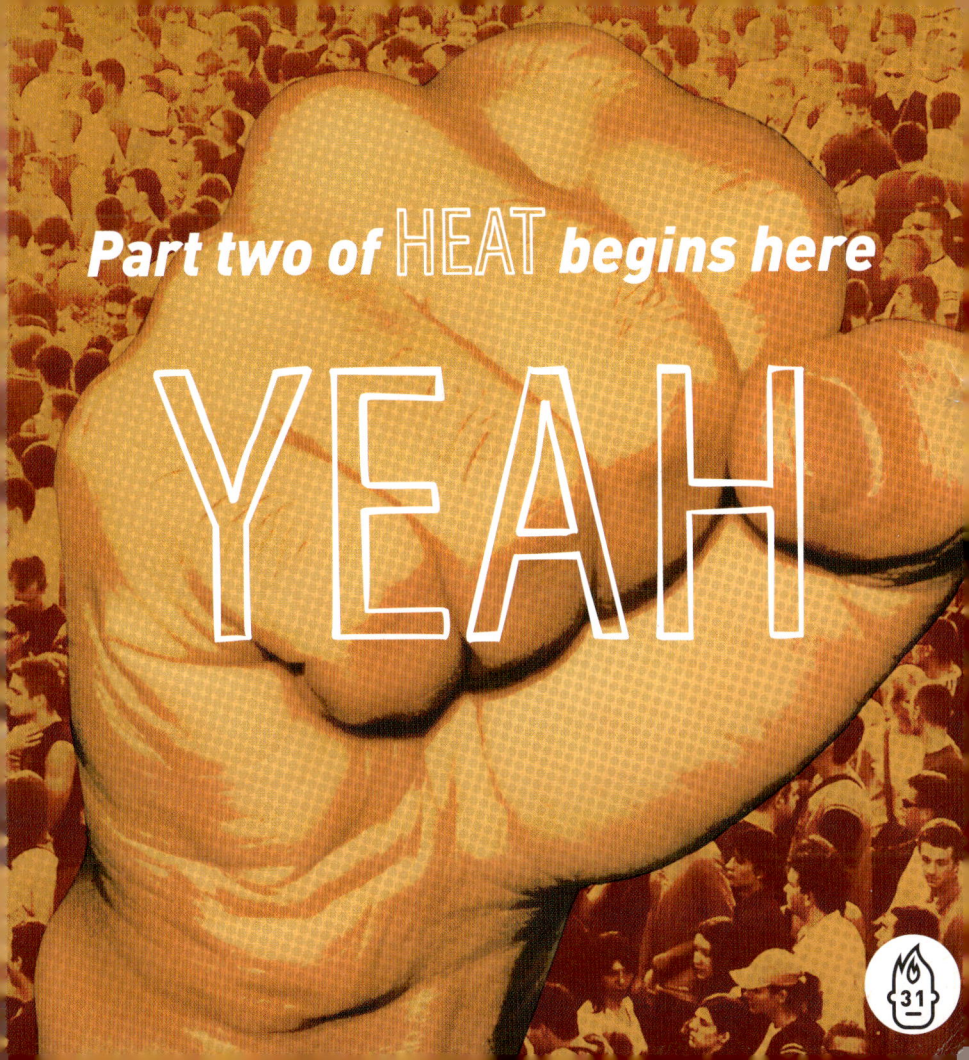

YEAH

"The man and his wife were both naked, and they felt no shame." **GENESIS 2:25**

Did you catch that? That's the Bible, you know—the Holy Scriptures, the "Good Book." It says that Adam and Eve were totally...

NUDE

To truly understand what God thinks of sex, you've got to imagine the Garden of Eden like you've never pictured it before. Forget those pictures you've seen in Sunday school where all the risky bits are all covered by fig leaves. Adam and Eve stood before each other stark naked. We don't know exactly how old they were—they were both brand-new creations, so really they were ageless. Think of them as in their perfect prime of life. Maybe Adam and Eve looked like naked seventeen-year-olds.